WARRIOR
IRON AND RUST

by Catherine Chambers
Illustrated by Martin Bustamante

HUNGRY
TOMATO™

WARRIOR
IRON AND RUST

Thanks to the creative team:

Senior Editor: Alice Peebles

Design: www.collaborate.agency

Consultant: John Haywood

First published in Great Britain in 2015
by Hungry Tomato Ltd
PO Box 181
Edenbridge
Kent, TN8 9DP

A CIP catalogue record for this book is
available from the British Library.

ISBN 978-1-910684-32-0

Printed and bound in China

Discover more at
www.hungrytomato.com

CONTENTS

INTRODUCING METAL WEAPONS

Most metals are tough and easily shaped and sharpened. Blacksmiths and swordsmiths could smelt, mould, hammer and grind bronze, iron and steel to make the deadliest handheld weapons. Some were thick, heavy bludgeoning instruments. Others were slender, fine, lethally sharp spikes and blades. Yet others could hook a knight off his horse or pin him to the ground. From fine arrowheads to slashing swords, sharp metal weapons carried by soldiers dominated warfare until modern times.

WEAPONS AND ARMOUR

A spear or arrow has a head with a tip, attached to an arm, or shaft.

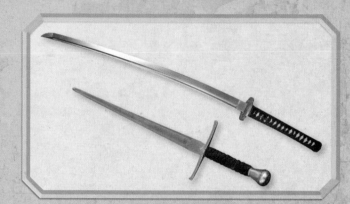

A sword or dagger has a blade with a sharp tip at the end. The handle is called a hilt, often ending in a ball-shaped pommel. The hilt's cross guard is known as a quillon.

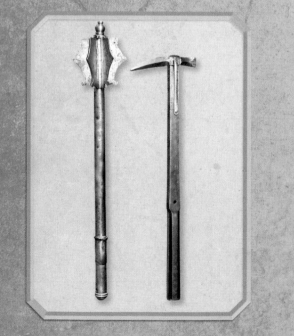

A mace (above left), axe or hammering weapon has a head attached to a handle, or haft.

Mail was the earliest form of armour for a medieval knight. It consisted of tens of thousands of interlocking metal rings woven together to form a shirt or hauberk for the body and a coif for the head.

PERSONAL PROTECTION

Armour strengthened as metal weapons became more deadly. Metal weapons became even more deadly as armour strengthened! Mail made from small metal links enabled the soldier to move with some ease. But a sword tip, dagger or arrow could force its way through.

Plate armour (right) began to replace mail from about 1200. Shaped from sheets of metal, it gave better protection against crush injuries. But the articulated joints made to fit the limbs could still be pierced by a sharp weapon. Shields might be bashed or unhooked from a soldier's arm. Battleaxes, hammers and flails were used to bludgeon helmets – and heads.

TOP TRAINING

Training with a lance included attacking a dummy and shield tied high on a swinging pole. The trainee galloped in fast and tried to hit the target hard.

SUPER SKILLS

Pikes were heavy, with 75 per cent of their weight held in front. A soldier had to develop his strength to hold the pike straight, without letting it dip.

MIGHTY MATERIALS

The heavy, tapered pole shaft was made from a strong wood such as ash. Near its end, the shaft was often strengthened further with iron sleeves, called cheeks.

FEROCIOUS FACTS

- The pike's length ranged from 2 to 6.5 m (6 to 21ft).

- Pike heads might have a deadly tip, axe head and hook.

- Sharp lance points could pierce plate armour.

PIERCING PIKES AND LANCES

The pike was a long, savage spear in use from the earliest times. Its extreme length enabled a soldier to make the first strike. Then, its razor-sharp steel, leaf-shaped tip wounded an opponent viciously and often fatally. Soldiers marched or ran with their pikes in close formation, called a phalanx, as here. Like a massive, surging bed of nails, the phalanx stopped the enemy in its tracks. A spear wielded by fast-moving cavalry was called a lance. At speed, this weapon could inflict a deadly wound or knock an opponent from his horse.

WHERE
Europe, Asia, North Africa

WHEN
300BCE to 1600s – based on earlier spears used worldwide

- Metal tips in various shapes, all very hard and sharp
- Shaft or pole of hardwood

LETHAL LONGBOW

The English longbow fired sharp, barbed iron arrows far and fast. The bow was so strong that an arrow could kill from 274 m (900 ft). The longbow's strength lay in its height. At 1.8 m (6 ft), it was as tall as a man, and its long string could be pulled back like a powerful catapult. Thin arrows pierced straight through a soldier's mail, while broader, heavier arrows flew farther and higher into a line of approaching infantry or cavalry. In battle, thousands of archers might advance in rows, raining down a storm of arrows on their enemy. More often, they fought defensively behind a line of sharpened stakes.

- Bow stave, often made of yew
- Hemp or flax bowstring
- Feather fletchling or flight to stabilize the arrow

TOP TRAINING

A longbow archer needed to draw the bow back with a force of up to 80 kg (180 lb). His backbone became bent and twisted after years of fighting.

SUPER SKILLS

It took years for an archer to learn longbow skills. England's King Edward 1 (1239–1307) forced his archers to practise every Sunday, banning all sports.

MIGHTY MATERIALS

Wrought-iron arrowheads could be sharpened into a razor-thin blade. These were attached to shafts carved from stout ash, oak or birch wood. A single piece of yew made the best bows, as there were no weak joins.

FEROCIOUS FACTS

- A longbow's 0.9-m (3-ft) arrows shot straight through a body.

- An archer could fire 12 longbow arrows a minute.

- At the Battle of Agincourt (1415), English longbowmen felled 10,000 Frenchmen in half an hour.

TOP TRAINING

A young knight practised by thrusting and slashing a pell, or stout wooden post, set firmly into the ground. He learned how to angle and strike with both edges of the blade.

SUPER SKILLS

A soldier with a longsword had no free arm to help balance his body as he thrust and cut. Instead, he developed strength in his legs and upper body for greater control.

MIGHTY MATERIALS

The longsword was very tough. A swordsmith fired and hammered strips of iron continually to strengthen them. He gave the sword balance by varying the width and thickness along the length of the blade.

FEROCIOUS FACTS

● The blade measured up to 122 cm (48 in), reaching from the floor to a soldier's chest.

● It could sever a limb or head in one stroke.

● The hilt's pommel and quillon were used to bash the opponent.

LOPPING WITH LONGSWORDS

This savage sword was a foot soldier's or knight's close-combat weapon of war. It had a strong, straight, double-edged blade with a long reach and a pointed tip. But its main advantage over other swords was its extended hilt. This enabled the soldier to grip tightly with both hands, increasing his power and control. He thrust at and pierced the opponent's mail forcefully from a distance. Or he cut and sliced at plate armour and any exposed limb – or neck! He bore down on an opponent's weapon, knocking it out of his hands. The sword also allowed for fast, strong strikes with one hand by a fighter on horseback.

WHERE
Central and Northern Europe

WHEN
About 1250 to 1550

Pommel

Long grip for two hands

Cross guard or quillon

Double-edged blade for delivering single, dismembering cuts

SLICING WITH THE SZABLA

WHERE
Central Europe

WHEN
1600s to 1800s
– based on 6th-century
sabres from the Middle
East

A winged Polish hussar used one hand to slice and slash with his slender, shallow-curved szabla. Its blade's single, razor-sharp edge tapered to a long, double-edged pointed tip. Every part of the blade could cut deeply, while the hilt inflicted a bruising blow. The hilt was crucial to the success of this sword. Its curve made it easy to grip, which allowed the swordsman to deliver a very controlled, swift strike. The szabla might have a knuckle guard and thumb ring to protect the hand, and these could give an opponent's hand a hefty strike.

Strengthened join between blade and hilt

Curved blade with one sharp edge

Double-edged tip, 15–18 cm (6–7 in) long

TOP TRAINING

Training included slashing while balancing on a swift horse. On the ground, a soldier practised fast, short steps in all directions, learning to slice with the szabla from any angle. Keeping a straight back gave power to the strike.

SUPER SKILLS

Hussars changed their handgrip with lightning speed. They could suddenly push their thumb hard against the hilt, straightening the wrist, to deliver a fearsome strike.

MIGHTY MATERIALS

A szabla was made from fine, strong steel. The join between its hilt and blade was strengthened by two feather-shaped pieces of metal. The sword's long tip did not snap off easily.

FEROCIOUS FACTS

- The blade reached 85 cm (33 in), or from floor to hip, and could make a wide gash.

- Its curved edge inflicted 'moulinets' – painful circular cuts.

- Hussars wore wooden wings covered in feathers to create awe and fear.

TOP TRAINING

From five years old, Samurai trained constantly with weapons, concentrating on swift movement and perfect judgement of distance. Thrusting and hitting had to be done with pinpoint accuracy.

SUPER SKILLS

Gunsen were carried in a sheath, with the fan tips uppermost. In a sudden attack, a Samurai could withdraw the gunsen swiftly by its tips so that it unfolded, protecting his hand.

MIGHTY MATERIALS

War fans had between six and 13 sharpened metal or heavy wooden ribs held together with strong rivets. Gunsen could fold because the ribs were joined together with flexible paper.

FEROCIOUS FACTS

● Gunbai could span 51 cm (20 in) and kill with a blow.

● The gunsen's sharp paper folds inflicted cuts to the eyes.

● Samurai officers signalled secret tactics to their troops with their gunbai.

GASHING WITH THE GUNSEN AND GUNBAI

These Japanese war fans did more than keep samurai warriors cool! Gunsen were lightweight folding fans with sharp iron blades that could fend off stones, darts and other small missiles. A gunbai was larger, heavier and did not fold. It was designed as a fearsome defensive, controlling weapon. It parried, or blocked, a samurai opponent's sword. Or it dealt painful blows to the hand, elbow or shoulder, forcing an enemy to drop his weapon. Fans aimed at the body's pressure points could paralyse. Once disarmed, the enemy was open to the samurai's deadly attack.

WHERE
Japan

WHEN
1400s to 1800s

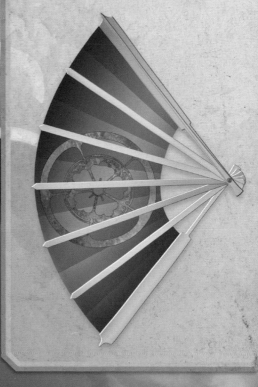

- Varying number of metal ribs

- Paper, sometimes lacquered, attached to the ribs for folding the gunsen

SLASHING WITH THE SHAMSHIR

WHERE
Persia
(now Iran)

WHEN
1200s to 1800s

This slender, curved, single-edged sword was designed to slash an opponent rather than pierce him. In Persian, 'shamshir' means 'lion's claw' and well describes this fearsome crescent-shaped sabre. Its strong central spine and long, tapering tip enabled the swordsman to slice with force. The lightweight shamshir was the Persian cavalry's deadliest single-handed weapon. Worn at the hip, it was drawn from a scabbard hung from two slings. It was perfect for fast-moving, mounted warfare, as it could be swung at enemy foot soldiers and cavalry in sweeping, carving movements.

... Inlaid hilt

Strong spine

Pronounced curve to the blade

Extended tip

TOP TRAINING

The sons of Persia's warrior class trained from an early age to ride horses and learn swordsmanship. They perfected the technique of angling the sharp shamshir blade to inflict a deep slice.

SUPER SKILLS

An expert swordsman could aim accurately and fatally at the neck and around the waist near the kidneys. He could strike backwards as well as forwards.

MIGHTY MATERIALS

The best 'wootz' steel from Damascus was used to make the finest blades. Wootz steel is also called watered steel because of its shimmering look. Gold, silver and ivory inlays decorated the hilt.

FEROCIOUS FACTS

- The blade was up to 0.9 m (3 ft) long.
- It could chop at bones as well as slice at flesh.
- The curved pommel gave a firm grip for a powerful hit.

TOP TRAINING

The young sons of samurai attended special combat schools. Vital skills included withdrawing and controlling the katana, standing with balanced readiness and glaring at the enemy.

SUPER SKILLS

Swordsmen could reverse the blade at great speed to strike from left to right, as well as right to left. A sudden thrust straight at the throat could surprise an enemy – fatally.

MIGHTY MATERIALS

Skilled swordsmiths heated and hammered together four layers of metal to make the blade. They used a tough but brittle steel for the razor-sharp edge. Layers of hard iron prevented the katana from bending, while a softer layer stopped it breaking.

FEROCIOUS FACTS

● The blade could measure up to 72 cm (28.5 in), or from floor to mid-thigh.

● The sloping, tapered tip enabled a complete gash to be made from head to stomach.

● A plaited cord around the hilt gave a firm grip to allow for a ferocious slash.

CUTTING WITH THE KILLER KATANA

This slender, two-handed sword was the main battle weapon of ruling samurai warriors. Its slightly curved, vicious single-edged blade and sloping point were designed to slice in a circular, sweeping motion. A mounted samurai could draw the sword at great speed from a sash belt tied around the waist. The blade was held uppermost, so with one slick, quick movement he could grasp the hilt and slash the enemy. The hilt was straight and long, easily gripped with both hands.

WHERE
Japan

WHEN
1100s to 1800s

..... Extended grip for two hands

Circular or squared cross guard

Slightly curved blade made from layers of metal

WHACKING WITH THE WAR HAMMER

WHERE
Eastern, Central and Northern Europe

———◆———

WHEN
1200s to 1400s – based on earlier Asian weapons

The foot soldiers of medieval armies wielded this fearsome, heavy weapon. Its purpose was to bash in helmets and breastplates, once plated armour became more widely used. A single blow from the hammerhead could knock an enemy unconscious, even through his helmet. It could splinter his skull, causing severe brain damage, and kill him. The sharp end or spike could tangle a horse's reins or unhook a knight's weapons, throwing him to the ground. It might also pierce thinner metal joints, as well as mail and unprotected flesh. The war hammer's haft was also used defensively, to block a sword strike, as here.

Heavy metal head

Sharp end for grappling with reins, stirrups and shields

Haft reinforced with metal

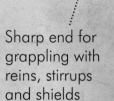

TOP TRAINING

To aim accurately at a moving head with a long-hafted hammer meant that soldiers had to practise hitting a small target while running. They used lightweight wooden hammers to practise against fellow soldiers.

SUPER SKILLS

A skilled soldier could switch swiftly from hammer to blade. He developed strength in his arms, so he could wield the war hammer with one hand, and another weapon with the other.

MIGHTY MATERIALS

Army blacksmiths smelted and moulded iron, steel or very heavy lead into a weighty head. The base of each head had a hole, or eye, into which the wooden haft was tightly wedged.

FEROCIOUS FACTS

- Handles ranged from 30 cm (12 in) to 152 cm (5 ft). A longer haft had a shattering force.

- The wooden haft was reinforced with metal or leather to blunt or damage an enemy's sword.

TOP TRAINING

Trainees bashed their flail against a small target or moving dummy. Then they practised against each other using a lightweight wooden version of the weapon.

SUPER SKILLS

The end of a knight's flail was either a baton or a spiked ball. The knight swung it constantly with outstretched arms so it did not come back and hit him.

MIGHTY MATERIALS

Blacksmiths added a steel safety chain to the head of a knight's flail. This stopped it from flying off like an uncontrolled missile.

FEROCIOUS FACTS

• Two-handed flails were the height of a soldier, up to 1.8 m (6 ft).

• Some flail heads were star shaped, capable of ripping flesh.

• Peasants used their threshing flails as offensive weapons to protect their fields from crop-raiders and land-grabbers.

FAST, FATAL FLAIL

This vicious, two-handed battering weapon was based on a peasant's powerful threshing tool. Sometimes, peasants fought with it very effectively for their lord or king. The flail's spiked or knobbed baton end was connected by a chain or leather thong to a long haft. This free movement allowed the weapon end to swing with great speed and force. A fast, accurate aim could kill with a single blow. The baton could hook around weapons, shields or even knights, dragging them to the ground.

WHERE
Europe

WHEN
1200s to 1500s – based on earlier Asian weapons

Baton with metal studs to cause extra damage

Chain attachment

Two-handed haft, about 1.8 m (6 ft) long

25

BEASTLY MEDIEVAL BATTLEAXE

WHERE
Worldwide

WHEN
800s to 1500s
– based on prehistoric
agricultural tools

These savage axes were sleek and sturdy chopping weapons. Their broad, crescent-shaped blades could slice or sever limbs, halting an enemy in his tracks. A single blow could pierce a helmet, plate armour or shield, or chop off a head. There were single- and double-handed battleaxes, with short, long, and even longer pole hafts. Some had a blade with a curved hammer or pick shape on the other side. The battleaxe was a common weapon of the foot soldier but a knight might tuck a small one in his belt.

• Iron axe head with decorative patterning

• Long haft, inserted into a socket in the butt end of the axe head

TOP TRAINING

Most foot soldiers used an axe from an early age, for chopping wood. Later, they practised accurate, swift slicing and throwing, probably at tree trunks or wood blocks.

SUPER SKILLS

Skilled soldiers could hook their battleaxe around swords, shields, plate armour and horses' reins – and around their opponents' legs and ankles to pull them off balance.

MIGHTY MATERIALS

Blacksmiths cast iron battleaxe heads in moulds. They then tempered, or softened, the edge with further heating. This made the blade less brittle. Most hafts were wooden, though some were iron.

FEROCIOUS FACTS

- A short haft of 30 cm (12 in) was perfect for close-combat chopping.

- The halberd was a doubly fierce combination of pike and battleaxe.

- Many battleaxes could be thrown together up to 12 m (40 ft) in a rain of axe heads.

WARS AND WARRIORS

Victory in battle and even in war has often been due to the strength and devastating use of metal weapons, and clever tactics.

PERFECT PIKE FORMATION

One of the most effective tacticians to use the phalanx formation was Epaminondas (about 410–362BCE). This great general and ruler from the central Greek city of Thebes used it to shatter Sparta's hold over the Greek city-states. His breakthrough came at the Battle of Leuctra in 371BCE. He adopted the new deep phalanx formation but used a massive 50 rows of hoplites. His greatest innovation, though, was to place these elite troops on the left flank, traditionally the weaker side. The Spartans came at them from their own stronger, right flank. They were impaled by the phalanx of pikes and Epaminondas's centre units and right flank cleaned up the rest.

SAVED BY THE WAR FAN

The gunsen and gunbai war fans were weapons of defence as much as attack. They often saved the life of a cornered samurai. This is what happened during the Fourth Battle of Kawanakajima in central Japan, in 1561. It took place between two rival military leaders, Takeda Shingen and Uesugi Kenshin. Thundering ahead on his horse, Kenshin had ridden right through the enemy cavalry. He headed straight for Shingen and thrust his sword at him with great force. But Shingen quickly raised his war fan and deflected the strike. For his great fighting skills, Shingen was known as the Tiger of Kai.

LEARNING LONGBOW TACTICS

England's 9th Earl of Warwick, William de Beauchamp (1237–1298), was a skilful military leader who appreciated the strengths of the longbow. Others did not. They preferred the crossbow, which shot lethal bolts straight and with lightning speed. But the Earl showed the longbow's worth during one of England's many attempts to crush their neighbours, the Welsh. At the night-time Battle of Maes Moydog in 1295, the Earl drove his cavalry hard at the Welsh, forcing them into small defensive units. Then he unleashed a heavy shower of longbow arrows, killing many and dispersing the rest. This was one of the early battles that used the longbow to its best advantage.

SUCCESS WITH THE SZABLA

The razor-sharp szabla finished off the Polish hussars' many enemies. This highly trained cavalry carried various weapons. They would charge hard at their enemy, screaming and with their armour flashing, then strike with their 5.8-m (19-ft) lightweight lances. The hussars followed this by shooting their opponents with pistols or stabbing them with daggers. They delivered single, fatal strikes with the szabla. This strategy led to many successes for the Polish hussars. In 1581 at the Battle of Kircholm, 1,000 hussars charged into 4,000 Swedish infantry, and even cannon! The powerful Swedish army was defeated and cut to bits.

MASTER SWORD FIGHTER

Miyamoto Musashi (1584–1645) was a famous samurai warrior known also as a 'kensai' or sword saint. He aimed to perfect the art and technique of the killer katana. Miyamoto fought and won at least 60 combats, slicing to death most of his opponents. This master sword fighter was not content with using just one sword to slash at his enemy. He developed the terrifying technique of *nito ichi-ryu*, wielding a katana in one hand and a short sword in the other. Sometimes Musashi threw the short sword at his opponent, then attacked with the killer katana.

MORE FEROCIOUS FACTS

- Hoplites' spearheads became much heavier in the 4th century. A metal butt at the other end of the haft was needed to balance the spearhead. The butt could also be used as a weapon.

- Horses were often severely wounded or even killed by spears. So in the 4th century, the Byzantine Army protected them with plate armour, just like their cavalrymen.

- At the Battle of Leuctra in 371 BCE, 1,000 mighty Spartans were piked to death by 6,000 Theban hoplites. This marked the beginning of the downfall of Sparta.

- The longbow fired some lethal arrowheads. The most damaging was the hardened steel broadhead arrow. It could be cast with two to four blade edges that ripped into the foe's flesh causing massive bleeding.

- The mace was used by priests! They were allowed to hit armoured knights as long as no bleeding occurred. An image of the Bishop of Bayeux clutching a mace appears on the Bayeux Tapestry in France. The artwork depicts England's defeat by the French in the Battle of Hastings in 1066.

- Knights did not care about their enemies' horses and pounded their legs with a war hammer to make them fall.

- A heavy war hammer from the Middle East called the horseman's pick was not designed to hurt horses. Its long spike end was rammed into enemy armour, or thrown.

- At the Battle of Crécy in 1346, English longbowmen faced French crossbow bolts and charging cavalry. But they held their ground, piercing and killing about 12,000 Frenchmen and their allies.

- In 1879, Zulu warriors in South Africa defeated British soldiers at the Battle of Isandhlwana. The British soldiers were heavily outnumbered but they had rifles, rockets and mountain guns. The Zulus used spears and a few old muskets. So in skilled hands, ancient metal weapons could be successful, even in more recent times.

GLOSSARY

BARBED
Having sharp, hooked tips

CAVALRY
Soldiers on horseback

CROSSBOW
Horizontal bow that shoots bolts straight at an enemy

HILT
Sword handle and pommel

HOPLITE
Ancient Greek pikeman

INFANTRY
Foot soldier

MOUNTAIN GUN
A gun that can be dismantled and transported uphill

PHALANX
Rows of soldiers holding pikes in close formation

PLATE ARMOUR
Body armour made from smooth plates of steel

PRESSURE POINT
A point on the body that feels pain or numbness when pressed hard

SAMURAI
Japanese warrior

SCABBARD
A sheath for holding a sword

SHAFT
The arm of an arrow or spear

WINGED HUSSARS
Heavily armed Polish cavalry who wore wings to look more fearsome

INDEX

THE AUTHOR

Catherine Chambers was born in Adelaide, South Australia, grew up in the UK and studied African History and Swahili at the School of Oriental and African Studies in London. She has written about 130 books for children and young adults, and enjoys seeking out intriguing facts for her non-fiction titles, which cover history, cultures, faiths, biography, geography and the environment.

THE ILLUSTRATOR

Martin Bustamante is an illustrator and painter from Argentina. As a teenager, he found new and fascinating worlds full of colour, shape and atmosphere in movies like *Star Wars* and the comic strip *Prince Valiant*, and these became his inspiration for drawing. Martin became a professional illustrator and has worked on books and magazines in Argentina, the USA and Europe.

Picture Credits (abbreviations: t = top; b = bottom; c = centre; l = left; r = right)

© www.shutterstock.com: 6 tl, 6 tr, 6 bl, 6 br, 7tc, 7br

Contents

BANG!!!

What makes things go BANG? Or crash, clatter, squeak, creak, hoot or any other sound? The answer is movement. Sound is a kind of energy that comes from things moving and shaking quickly to and fro – also known as vibrating.

TA-TA-TAAAAA

WHIZZZZZ

RAT-A-TAT RAT-A-TAT

RUMBLE RUMBLE

WHIZZY SCIENCE

Make it Bang!

Written by:
Anna Claybourne

Illustrated by:
Kimberley Scott and Venetia Dean

Published in paperback in 2014 by Wayland
Copyright © Wayland 2014

Wayland
338 Euston Road
London NW1 3BH

Wayland Australia
Hachette Children's Books
Level 17/207
Kent Street
Sydney, NSW 2000

Senior Editor: Julia Adams
Designer: Anthony Hannant (LittleRedAnt)
Illustrator (step-by-steps): Kimberley Scott
Illustrator (incidentals and final crafts): Venetia Dean
Proofreader & Indexer: Sara Harper

Dewey categorisation: 534

ISBN 978 0 7502 8370 0

Printed in China

1 3 5 7 9 10 8 6 4 2

Wayland is a division of Hachette Children's Books,
an Hachette UK company.
www.hachette.co.uk

Picture acknowledgements:
All photographs: Shutterstock; except: p. 17: iStockphoto.

WHIZZZZ

ZIP

LIKE WHAT?

Things vibrate in different ways to make all kinds of sounds.

BANG! If you bang a door shut, it vibrates suddenly, making a loud, short noise.

CRASH! Hitting a cymbal makes the metal vibrate with a loud crashing sound.

Laaaaaa! When you sing or talk, you blow air through stringy bits of muscle in your throat, and they vibrate.

INTO YOUR EARS

Of course, we only know what all these sounds are like because we can hear them. They spread out through the air and go into our ears, which are specially built to detect them. Hearing is amazingly useful – it helps us talk to each other, send long-distance messages, spot danger, and enjoy TV, films and music.

Sound wave

BEING A SCIENTIST

This book is packed full of fun experiments to try with bangs, crashes and other sounds, to help you find out how sounds work. To get the best results, here are a few sound science tips:

1. Set up your experiments according to the instructions and watch carefully to see what happens.

2. To be like a real scientist, write down your results in a notebook.

3. Scientists often do experiments several times over, to check they always work the same way.

see a bang

Everything that makes a sound is moving, but you can't always see the vibrations that make sound. This experiment makes it a bit easier to spot them!

YOU WILL NEED

1) An empty food container
2) Clingfilm or a plastic bag
3) Long elastic bands
4) A pencil or wooden spoon
5) Rice grains

Here's What to Do...

1. Remove the lid from your food container.

2. Stretch a large piece of the plastic bag tightly around the container, and hold it in place with elastic bands.

3. Sprinkle a pinch of rice onto the surface of your 'drum'.

4. Bang the drum gently with a pencil or wooden spoon.

WHAT'S GOING ON?

When you hit the drum, it makes the plastic skin vibrate very quickly up and down. It's hard to see, because the vibrations are quite small and fast. But if there are rice grains sitting on top, the vibrations make them jump up and down, showing you what's happening.

TROUBLESHOOTER

The plastic should be very tight and smooth. You may need two people to put it on – one to hold it while the other fixes it in place.

WHAT NEXT?

Do the rice grains behave differently if you put them near the edge or right in the middle?

Try making a loud noise just above the drum without touching it (shout, clap or bang things together) – can you make the rice grains jump? Why does this happen?

Bang, twang, pop

Try making some loud and peculiar noises using some of the everyday objects around you. See if you can work out why they sound different from each other.

YOU WILL NEED
1) Wooden blocks, bricks or chopping boards
2) A ruler
3) A balloon
4) A coin with lots of sides (a screw nut with six sides also works)

1. Clap your hands, stamp your feet, or bang two blocks of wood together.

2. Put your finger in your mouth, close it tightly, blow hard, then pop your finger out sideways.

3. Hold a ruler firmly over the edge of a table, and twang the free end.

4. Put a multi-sided coin inside a balloon, blow it up and tie it, then twirl it around to make the coin roll fast around the inside.

8

WHAT'S GOING ON?

All these activities involve hitting or somehow moving an object to make it vibrate. The sound the object makes depends on how it moves, and what it is made of. Springy or rubbery objects such as the ruler and the balloon skin tend to make more twangy, long-lasting sounds, as they bounce to and fro. Hard, rigid objects such as wooden blocks stop vibrating more quickly, and make short, sharp sounds.

Can you make a hooting owl sound with your hands? Cup them together, with a gap between your thumbs, and blow gently across the gap.

DID YOU KNOW?

If there is air inside a vibrating object, the air will vibrate too, adding to the sound.

WHAT NEXT?

Write down descriptions of each sound – are they high or low, loud or quiet, spooky, funny or strange?

How a bang travels

Why can we hear sound? Because it travels from the moving object to our ears, in the form of sound waves. This experiment shows how sound waves work.

YOU WILL NEED

1) A metal or plastic slinky or spiral spring toy
2) A smooth, hard floor
3) At least two people

Here's What to Do...

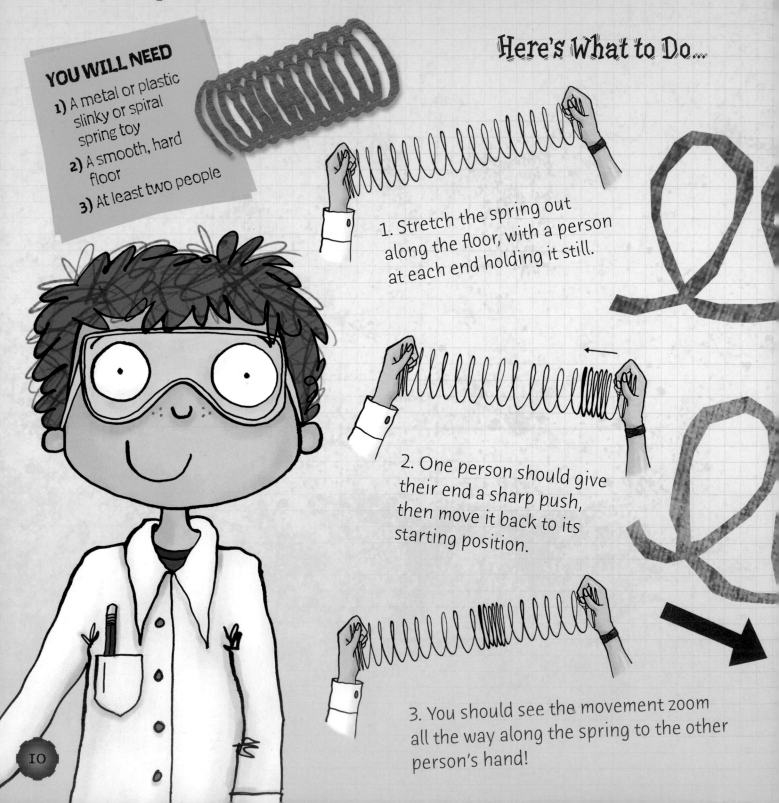

1. Stretch the spring out along the floor, with a person at each end holding it still.

2. One person should give their end a sharp push, then move it back to its starting position.

3. You should see the movement zoom all the way along the spring to the other person's hand!

WHAT'S GOING ON?

When you push the end of the spring, the first coil pushes the next coil, which pushes the next one, and so on. In this way the energy of the push moves right along the spring.

 TROUBLESHOOTER

The spring needs to be spread out, but not pulled too tight; experiment to find the best amount of stretch.

Sound waves in air work the same way. When something vibrates, it pushes against the tiny molecules in the air around it, making them vibrate too. They push the molecules next to them, and they push the molecules next to them, and so on.

BOUNCING BACK

An echo is a sound wave that has bounced off a surface. If you can tape one end of your spring to a wall, you may be able to recreate this, too.

WHAT NEXT?

Can you send a series of waves all at once, one following another?

Can you recreate how a sound wave travels using a line of people?

The speed of a bang

You hit a drum or shut a door, and you hear a sound – BANG! It seems as if it happens straight away. But actually it takes time for sound to travel to your ears. So how fast does it go?

YOU WILL NEED

1) A tape measure or measuring wheel
2) Two bin lids, pan lids or cymbals
3) A stopwatch
4) A pen and paper
5) A calculator
6) At least two people

Here's What to Do...

1. Measure out a 250 m distance on a flat playing field, park or beach.

250 m

2. One person should stand 250 m away from the other, and bang the lids or cymbals together.

3. The other person should start the timer when they see the bang happening, and stop it when they hear the bang. You'll need to react quickly!

4. Write down how long the bang takes to travel 250 m. From this you can calculate the speed of sound (see What's Going On?).

WHAT'S GOING ON?

When the lids bang, the sound starts to spread out through the air. You see it happen almost immediately, as the speed of light is very, very fast. But sound is much slower. If you are 250 m away, it should take about 0.7 seconds to reach you.

To find the speed of sound in metres per second, divide 250 by your result.

For example, 250 divided by 0.73 = about 342 metres per second.

This is the same as about 1,235 kilometres per hour (or 768 miles per hour) – as fast as a very fast jet plane. Zoom!

! TROUBLESHOOTER

You need a calm day – avoid noisy wind and rain!

THUNDER AND LIGHTNING

In a thunderstorm, thunder makes the sound of lightning. But if the storm is far away, you see the lightning first, then hear the CRACK! when the sound reaches you.

WHAT NEXT?

Do the experiment several times to get a good average measurement.

Can you do it over an even bigger distance?

Bangs and whispers

Why are some sounds loud and others quiet? Try making sounds of different volumes and see if you can work out what's happening.

Here's What to Do...

YOU WILL NEED
1) A drum and drumstick, or a pan and a wooden spoon
2) Musical instruments, if you have any
3) Everyday objects
4) A pen and paper

1. Try making loud and quiet bangs on your drum or pan.

2. Try making loud and quiet sounds on a musical instrument or by singing.

3. Try clapping, rubbing objects together, or rattling a box with something inside.

4. Write down what you have to do to make sound louder in each experiment.

WHAT'S GOING ON?

Whatever you're using to make a sound, making it louder always involves the same thing. Did you notice what it was? Sound is a form of energy, and louder sounds carry more energy, as they involve stronger vibrations. So to make louder sounds, you have to put more energy in. That means hitting, blowing or shaking harder. Put in a lot less energy, and you get a really quiet sound instead.

SOUND SCALE

Scientists measure how loud sounds are using the decibel or dB scale. Very quiet sounds, like rustling leaves, measure about 20 dB. Super-loud sounds like a jet taking off are around 140 dB.

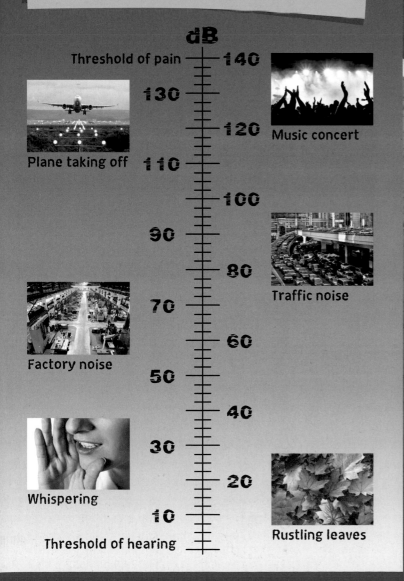

dB

Threshold of pain — 140

130

Plane taking off

120 — Music concert

110

100

90

80 — Traffic noise

Factory noise

70

60

50

40

Whispering

30

20 — Rustling leaves

10

Threshold of hearing

WHAT NEXT?

Experiment with the plastic drum skin and rice grains from page 6. Do the rice grains behave differently when you bang the drum skin harder?

Whispering is another way to be quiet, but to do this, you stop your voice from making a sound, and just use your breath. How quietly can you talk without whispering?

The Screaming cup

How can you make a cup shriek and squawk like a parrot? It might seem pretty unlikely, but here's how to do it...

YOU WILL NEED
1) A clean, dry paper cup
2) A sharp pencil
3) A candle
4) Thread

Here's What to Do...

1. Make a small hole in the base of the cup, using a sharp pencil (ask an adult to help).

2. Cut a 30-cm long piece of thread and thread it through the hole, then knot the end so it's held in place.

"Squawk!"

3. Rub the candle up and down the thread to make it waxy.

4. Hold the cup in one hand, and pull on the thread with the other, so that your hand slips down it.

WHAT'S GOING ON?

As your fingers slip down the thread in sudden jerks and jumps, they make it vibrate. The vibrations are small and you would normally hardly hear anything. But as the thread is connected to the cup, it makes the cup vibrate too, along with the air inside it. This makes a louder sound... ...which sounds a bit like a squawking parrot!

squawk!

PAPER CUP PHONE CALL

A paper cup telephone works in the same way. You use a long piece of string to join two cups together, then stretch it tight. When you speak into one cup, the vibrations travel along the string and into the other cup, making it sound as if the other person is right next to you!

AMPLIFICATION

Making sounds louder is called amplifying them.

TROUBLESHOOTER

If it doesn't work, try gripping the thread with a damp paper towel.

WHAT NEXT?

What happens if you put the cup to your ear and tap the bottom of it?

Try cutting the bottom off a paper cup and speaking through it.

High and low

How high or low a sound is, is called its pitch. Every sound has a pitch, and musical instruments and voices can change their pitch. How do they do it?

Here's What to Do...

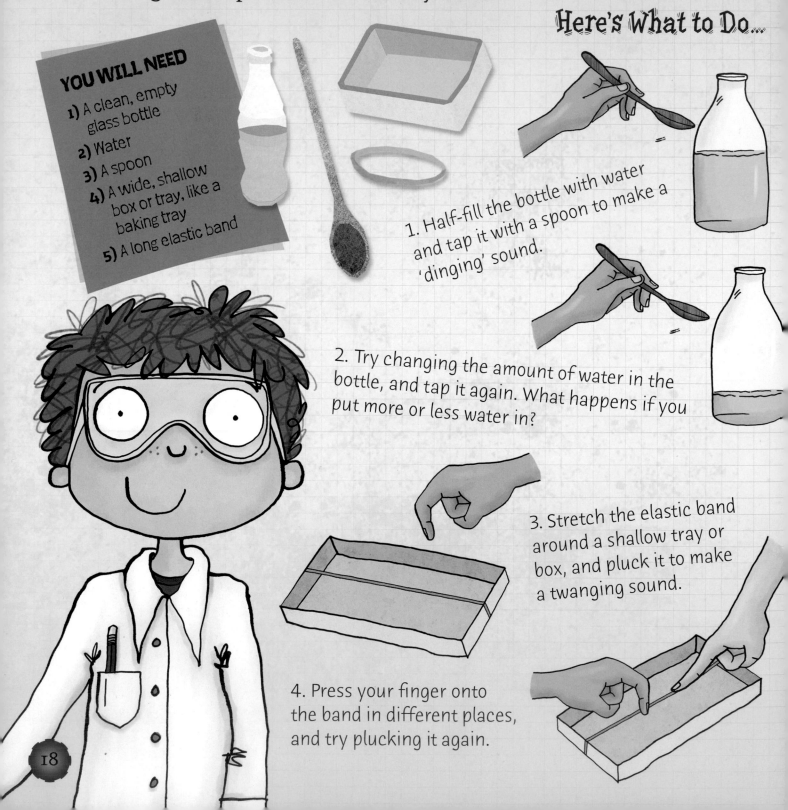

YOU WILL NEED

1) A clean, empty glass bottle

2) Water

3) A spoon

4) A wide, shallow box or tray, like a baking tray

5) A long elastic band

1. Half-fill the bottle with water and tap it with a spoon to make a 'dinging' sound.

2. Try changing the amount of water in the bottle, and tap it again. What happens if you put more or less water in?

3. Stretch the elastic band around a shallow tray or box, and pluck it to make a twanging sound.

4. Press your finger onto the band in different places, and try plucking it again.

WHAT'S GOING ON?

With both these experiments, you are changing the pitch of a sound. You are actually doing this by making the vibrations faster or slower. When there's less air in the bottle, it makes shorter and faster vibrations, and a higher-pitched sound. When the elastic band is shorter, it vibrates to and fro faster, and its pitch is higher.

HOW MANY HERTZ?

Pitch is measured by the number of vibrations per second, also called Hertz, or Hz. For example, the top string on a guitar is about 330 Hz, meaning it vibrates 330 times every second – quite fast!

WHAT NEXT?

You can blow across the top of the bottles to make a different sound – but is it the same pitch?

If you have several bottles the same size and shape, you can use different amounts of water to 'tune' them to different notes, and make a bottle xylophone. What tunes can you play?

The Sounds of speech

You always have one musical instrument with you – your voice! Find out how you make it go up and down, and why.

Here's What to Do...

1. Put your fingers gently on your throat, like this.

2. Sing loudly, starting very low, and moving up to a high note, then back down.

3. Now change between singing a note, and blowing while making no sound.

Your voice is made by two bands of muscle in your throat called vocal cords or vocal folds. To make your voice higher, they stretch, so that they are tighter and vibrate faster. When you sing low, they are looser and vibrate more slowly. Parts of your throat have to move around to change their position, and you can feel this with your hand.

Vocal cords together make a sound.

TROUBLESHOOTER

You might need to move your hand around a bit at first to find the best position.

You can also move your vocal cords apart so that they don't vibrate at all. This happens when you blow, whisper or breathe normally. When they're together, you can feel the vibrations, but when they are apart, the vibrations stop.

WHAT NEXT?

Think about what pitch is for — why is it useful for our voices to go up and down?

Try speaking without changing pitch at all. It's hard!

Try saying one word, such as 'yes', 'no' or 'OK', but using pitch to give it different meanings — for example try to sound keen, bored or rude. See if other people understand you!

Vocal cords apart for breathing.

Solid sounds

Sounds travel differently through solid objects, such as spoons, string and fingers, than they do through the air. Find out what happens with this dangling, jangling spoon experiment!

YOU WILL NEED

1) String
2) A metal spoon
3) A table or other hard object

Here's What to Do...

1. Tie a 30-cm long piece of string to the handle of a metal spoon.

2. Wrap the other end of the string around your finger a few times, and bang the spoon gently against a table to make a ringing noise.

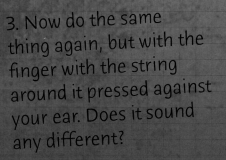

3. Now do the same thing again, but with the finger with the string around it pressed against your ear. Does it sound any different?

WHAT'S GOING ON?

When the sound just travels from the spoon through the air to your ears, it's quieter. When it travels along the spoon, the string and your finger into your ear, it sounds louder and a bit more detailed. Solid things actually carry sounds better and faster than air does.

There's a simple reason for this – solids contain more molecules than air, and they're more tightly packed together. This means sound vibrations pass from one molecule to the next more easily and quickly.

SAFETY WARNING

Press your finger gently against your ear, but DON'T stick it right inside – it's not very good for you.

Solid

Liquid

Gas

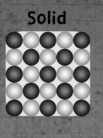

You could try this experiment with other solid objects, too, such as a ruler or a plastic cup. What works best?

FEELING FOR SOUNDS

Deaf people can sometimes get a better sense of sounds by touching the vibrating object to pick up the sound vibrations. Percussion player Evelyn Glennie, for example, performs with bare feet to help her sense vibrations through the ground.

WHAT NEXT?

What happens if you put your ears under the water in the bath while the tap is running? Sound also travels better through liquids than in air, as liquids have more molecules.

Stop that banging

Sometimes, you want to stop sound and keep it quiet. In fact, sometimes loud noises can be a problem. So what's the best way to block out sounds?

Here's What to Do...

YOU WILL NEED

1) Three tallish cardboard boxes
2) Cotton wool
3) Craft glue
4) Modelling clay
5) A small bell or whistle

1. Take one box and stick a thick layer of cotton wool all over the inside of it, using the glue.

2. Press a layer of modelling clay all over the inside of the second box.

3. Leave one box empty.

4. Ring a small bell or blow a whistle inside each box. Do they sound different?

24

WHAT'S GOING ON?

Sound bounces and echoes off some surfaces, but gets absorbed or soaked up by others. The softer and woollier the surface, the better it is at soaking up sound and making it seem quieter. We use this muffling effect for soundproofing – trying to stop unwanted sounds from spreading.

TROUBLESHOOTER

For it to work well the boxes should all be the same size.

BLOCK YOUR EARS!

Really loud sounds can damage your hearing, so people who work with loud noises need to protect their ears. Ear defenders like these block out sound with several layers of foam, wool or rubber.

Earplugs, made of squishy foam-like material, fit just inside the ears. Ear defenders sit over the top of your ears to block out sound.

WHAT NEXT?

What makes the best sound insulation? Try other materials too, such as cardboard, felt, tissue paper or a woolly sock.

When would sound insulation be useful? Think about where you would put it to keep a bedroom quiet at night, or stop the sounds of music escaping from a recording studio.

find the bang

Can you tell which direction a sound is coming from?
If you have two ears you can, and often do! How is
that possible?

YOU WILL NEED

1) A scarf or eye
mask to use as
a blindfold

2) A chair

3) A group of at least
four people

Here's What to Do...

1. One person should put
on the blindfold and sit in
the chair.

2. The others should stand in a ring around the
chair, and take turns to make a noise.

3. The listener should try to point to where each
noise is coming from.

WHAT'S GOING ON?

We use the fact that we have two ears to detect the direction of sounds. As sound takes time to travel, it reaches your ears at very slightly different times. You don't notice this, but your brain can tell! It uses the information to help it work out where sounds are coming from.

The outer part of your ear helps too. Its shape reflects sounds into your ear in different patterns depending on what direction they come from. Again, your brain can spot these tiny differences.

SATELLITE EARS

The sticking-out part of your ear, called the pinna, works a bit like a satellite dish to catch sounds and bounce them into your ears. It also protects your earhole from wind, rain and dirt!

TROUBLESHOOTER

Don't stand too close to the chair – stand back, a few steps away.

WHAT NEXT?

What happens if the person in the chair covers up one of their ears? Does the task become harder?

Take turns so that everyone has a go on the chair. Are some people better than others at spotting where sounds come from?

How musical are you?

Some people find it easy to listen to and remember tunes, while others find it almost impossible. Test yourself and your friends!

YOU WILL NEED

1) A piano, xylophone or electronic keyboard

2) A scarf or eye mask to use as a blindfold

Here's What to Do...

1. The person being tested should put on the blindfold and face away from the keyboard.

2. Play two different notes on the keyboard, fairly close together, one after the other.

3. Ask the listener if they know whether the notes have moved up or down in pitch.

4. If they get that right, ask them how many keys apart the notes were.

WHAT'S GOING ON?

The ability to hear tunes and different notes is partly in your genes, meaning you are born with it. It can also be affected by how much you have learned about music. However, a few people – around 4 out of every 100 – simply cannot do it, however hard they try! Their brains simply don't work that way.

! TROUBLESHOOTER

Make sure the blindfold doesn't cover the person's ears!

PERFECT PITCH

Some people have an ability called perfect pitch, which means they can actually name a particular note when they hear it.

WHAT'S THAT RACKET?

There are a few people who cannot understand musical sounds at all. To them, music just sounds like a jumble of noises, and some even find it upsetting. This condition is called amusia.

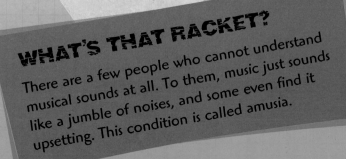

WHAT NEXT?

Test to see if anyone can sing the exact notes they have heard. If they can manage two notes easily, see if they can sing three, four or five in a row.

29

Glossary

amplify To make a sound louder.

amusia Inability to make sense of music.

decibel (dB) Unit used to measure how loud a sound is.

ear defenders Ear covers for blocking out loud sounds.

earplugs Small plugs that fit inside the ears to block out sounds.

echo Sound that has hit a surface and bounced off it.

energy The power to do work or make things happen.

Hertz (Hz) Unit used to measure pitch, or how high or low a sound is.

molecules The tiny units that materials are made of.

perfect pitch Ability to recognize and name musical notes by their sound.

pinna The sticking-out part of the ear that you can see.

pitch How high or low a sound is.

sound waves Patterns of sound vibrations that spread out through a substance.

soundproofing Muffling sound to stop it from spreading.

vibrate To shake very quickly to and fro.

vocal cords or vocal folds Bands of muscle in the throat that vibrate to make voice sounds.

further reading

BOOKS

Make and Use: Musical Instruments
by Anna-Marie D'Cruz, Wayland, 2010

Experiments with Sound and Hearing
by Chris Woodford, Gareth Stevens Publishing,
2010

Science Detective Investigates: Sound
by Harriet McGregor, Wayland, 2011

Bang! Sound And How We Hear Things
by Peter Riley, Franklin Watts, 2012

Amazing Science: Sound
by Sally Hewitt, Wayland, 2014

How Does Science Work: Sound
by Carol Ballard, Wayland, 2014

WEBSITES

Zoom Science: Sound
http://pbskids.org/zoom/activities/sci/#sound

Neuroscience for Kids: Hearing Experiments
http://faculty.washington.edu/chudler/chhearing.
html

Index